S0-BMV-246

GEESE FLY IN "V" FORMATION

EAGLE

VULTURE

HAWK →

FALCON

KESTREL

CRANE

HERON

EGRET

DUCKS FLY IN SMALL GROUPS WITH NO APPARENT LEADER.

THIS NATURE NOTEBOOK BELONGS TO:

_____

_____

_____

CROW

CORMORANT

GULL

TERN

PLOVER

SANDPIPER

IBIS

PELICAN

Copyright © 1997 by Jim Arnosky. All rights reserved under
International and Pan-American Copyright Conventions.
Published in the United States by Random House, Inc., New
York, and simultaneously in Canada by Random House of Canada
Limited, Toronto.
http://www.randomhouse.com/

Library of Congress Cataloging-in-Publication Data
Arnosky, Jim.
Bird watcher / by Jim Arnosky.
p.   cm. — (Jim Arnosky's nature notebooks)
SUMMARY: Briefly presents tips on bird watching, with blank
pages provided for keeping records of sightings.
ISBN 0-679-86716-3
1. Bird watching—Juvenile literature.
[1. Bird watching.
2. Nature study.]   I. Title.   II. Series: Arnosky, Jim.
Jim Arnosky's nature notebooks.
QL677.5.A76   1997   598'.07'234—dc20   96-21650

Printed in the United States of America   10 9 8 7 6 5 4 3 2 1

JIM ARNOSKY'S
NATURE NOTEBOOKS
BIRD WATCHER

Random House New York

BIRD WATCHING

In a way, all of us are bird watchers. We see birds in the air, on the ground, and on the water. We see them on our way to school or work. We watch them even when we are not looking for them.

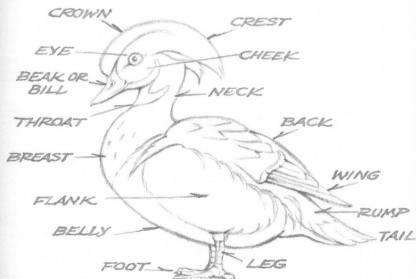

WHEN DESCRIBING BIRDS IN YOUR NOTES, USE THE PROPER TERMS.

CROWN
CREST
EYE
CHEEK
BEAK OR BILL
NECK
THROAT
BACK
BREAST
WING
FLANK
RUMP
BELLY
TAIL
FOOT
LEG

Some families of birds can adapt to almost any environment. For instance, sparrows can live in many different kinds of places—from city streets to wilderness areas. Other species have more particular habitat requirements. Woodpeckers thrive only where there are plenty of dead or dying trees for them to peck and dig into in search of wood-boring insects.

PILEATED WOODPECKER.

FINDING BIRDS

Look for birds around water, where they come to drink, bathe, or feed on water plants and insects. Look for birds near bushes and brush, in fields or woods, along roadsides—anywhere there is cover for them to hide or nest in. One thing is for certain: Wherever you are, wherever you go, you will find birds.

BIRDS ARE THE EASIEST
WILD ANIMALS TO FIND
AND WATCH. THEY ARE
CONSPICUOUS IN FLIGHT...

IDENTIFYING BIRDS

There are almost as many kinds of birds as there are places birds are found. There are perching birds, climbing birds, gliding birds, and soaring birds. There are ground birds, shore birds, and water birds. Many species of birds can be recognized by shape alone. The charts at the beginning and end of this book show the birds that are most easily recognized by shape.

. . . AND THEY DRAW ATTENTION TO THEMSELVES WITH THEIR CALLS AND SONGS.

FIELD MARKS

When you see a bird that cannot be readily identified by its shape or color, look for identifying patterns in its plumage. Any streaks, spots, large patches of color, or rings of color around the eyes or neck are called field marks. Some field marks, such as eye and neck rings or breast streaks, are visible all the time. Wing and tail field marks may be visible only when a bird's wing or tail feathers are spread. After a day afield, count how many different birds you identified by shape alone, and how many you recognized by their distinctive field marks.

*These days, the myrtle warbler is also known as the yellow-rumped warbler.

BOTH MALE AND FEMALE HOODED MERGANSERS HAVE CRESTS. AN ADDITIONAL FIELD MARK IS THE MALE'S BRIGHT WHITE "HOOD."

♀

♂

ANY BRIGHT PATCHES MAKE GOOD FIELD MARKS.

MYRTLE WARBLERS HAVE YELLOW RUMPS.*

CAPE PETREL

THE SOLITARY VIREO'S WHITE EYE RINGS ARE MORE SUBTLE FIELD MARKS.

SOMETIMES A BIRD'S MOST DISTINCTIVE FIELD MARK IS NOT A MARK AT ALL, BUT THE WAY IT HOLDS OR MOVES ITS TAIL.

RUDDY DUCKS OFTEN HOLD THEIR TAIL FEATHERS UPRIGHT.

PHOEBES HABITUALLY PUMP THEIR TAILS.

♂ = MALE   ♀ = FEMALE

11

RED-BREASTED NUTHATCH
PREPARING TO CRACK
OPEN A SEED ON A
BRANCH.

BIRD BEHAVIOR

CROW
ON
LOOKOUT

Bird watching is more than identifying the birds you see. It is also watching the things birds do—how they find food, how they use their bills or beaks to eat, and how they react to their natural enemies. Bird watching is finding out how different birds build their nests and raise their young. A bird watcher's notebook should be filled with observations of bird behavior.

PINE SISKINS
SHARING A
FEEDER.

NATURAL ENEMIES

Birds have many enemies. They must be vigilant to protect their young. For your safety and for the security of the birds, always stay at least ten feet from nesting birds. Use your binocular to see them up close. Never climb up a tree or stand on a ladder to look into a bird nest that is built high off the ground. Bird parents will swoop and dive at you to drive you away, and may cause you to lose your balance and fall. If you are on the ground looking up at a bird's nest and one or both of the parents begin diving at you, back away. You are obviously too close.

BARN SWALLOW
AND YOUNG

RECORDING BIRDS

Reserve at least one full page in your notebook for each bird sighting. Record the feature by which you identified the bird—its color, shape, or field mark. Then sketch a small picture of the bird the way it looked when you first noticed it. Next record the place you saw the bird. Was it in a field or near the water? Was it on a grassy lawn or in a woodlot? Make a quick sketch of the bird's habitat and draw the bird in it. Note what the bird was doing when you spotted it and the things it did while you were watching.

AUGUST 8, 1995   7:00 AM   AT THE POND

THIS MORNING I SAW A GREAT BLUE HERON IN THE CATTAIL CORNER OF THE POND.

AT FIRST IT HAD ITS NECK ALL SCRUNCHED DOWN AND I COULDN'T TELL WHAT BIRD IT WAS.

THEN IT STRETCHED TALL AND I COULD TELL IT WAS A HERON.

I WATCHED AS IT WAITED FOR A FISH AND I SAW IT CATCH ONE!

THE HERON SWALLOWED THE FISH WHOLE — HEAD FIRST.

THE FISH WAS SO BIG, IT MADE A BULGE IN THE HERON'S SKINNY NECK AS THE BIRD SLOWLY SWALLOWED IT DOWN.

15

YOUR NATURE NOTEBOOK

Your nature notebook is small and flexible so you can roll it up, put it in a pocket, and carry it wherever you go. But as small as it may be, it can hold many wonderful experiences. Take care to write small and fit a lot on every page. Detailed drawings of a bird, along with a brief description of the time and place, can all be included on one or two notebook pages.

I'll be dropping in on a few more pages throughout the rest of the book to tell you a little more about bird watching. Until then...

HAPPY BIRD WATCHING!

Jim Arnosky

MALES AND FEMALES ♂ ♀

IN MANY SPECIES OF BIRDS, MALES AND FEMALES LOOK ALIKE.

IN SPECIES WHERE MALES AND FEMALES DIFFER, EVEN SLIGHTLY, THE MORE COLORFUL OF THE PAIR IS THE MALE...

♀ ♂ MALE HAS RUBY THROAT

ONE EXCEPTION IS THE BELTED KINGFISHER. THE FEMALE BELTED KINGFISHER IS MORE COLORFUL THAN THE MALE.

FEMALE HAS AN ORANGE BELT.

♂ ♀

25

MANTLING

WHENEVER A BIRD SPREADS ITS WINGS AND LOWERS THEM TO THE GROUND, IT IS A SIGN OF AGGRESSION,

WHETHER TO DEFEND TERRITORY

OR TO HOARD FOOD.

THIS AGGRESSIVE ACTION IS KNOWN AS MANTLING.

RARE BIRD SIGHTINGS

IF YOU HAPPEN TO SEE A BIRD THAT
IS CONSIDERED RARE OR ENDANGERED,
DRAW A STAR ON AN UPPER CORNER
OF YOUR NOTEBOOK PAGE. THIS WILL
MARK THE DAY AS A SPECIAL ONE.

DON'T FORGET TO NOTIFY YOUR LOCAL
AUDUBON SOCIETY ABOUT ANY
RARE BIRD SIGHTINGS.

CHOOSE ONE RARE BIRD SPECIES
AS YOUR OWN PARTICULAR FAVORITE
AND ALWAYS KEEP AN EYE OUT FOR IT.

MY OWN PARTICULAR
FAVORITE IS THE
OSPREY.

HERE ARE THREE OTHER RARE
SPECIES TO LOOK FOR:

PEREGRINE
FALCON

BALD
EAGLE

IVORY-BILLED
WOODPECKER.
[OUR RAREST
BIRD !]

NOTE DOUBLE WHITE WING BARS

WAS THAT A HAWK OR A CROW?

THE MOST COMMONLY SEEN ROADSIDE BIRDS ARE HAWKS AND CROWS. SINCE HAWKS AND CROWS ARE NEARLY THE SAME SIZE, IT IS SOMETIMES HARD TO TELL WHICH IS WHICH.

HERE IS ONE SURE WAY TO DISTINGUISH A HAWK FROM A CROW, EVEN AT A DISTANCE:

A HAWK, LIKE ALL OTHER BIRDS OF PREY, CARRIES FOOD CLUTCHED IN ITS SHARP TALONS.

A CROW ALWAYS CARRIES FOOD IN ITS BILL.

SEE HOW MANY OTHER DIFFERENCES YOU CAN FIND BY OBSERVING THESE TWO COMMON ROADSIDE BIRDS.

53

ABOUT THE AUTHOR

Naturalist Jim Arnosky has written and illustrated over 35 nature books for children. His titles have earned numerous honors, including American Library Association Notable Book Awards and Outstanding Science Books for Children Awards presented by the National Science Teachers Association Children's Book Council Joint Committee. He has also received the Eva L. Gordon Award for Body of Work for his contribution to children's literature.

An all-around nature lover, Mr. Arnosky can often be found fishing, hiking, boating, or videotaping wildlife on safari. He lives with his family in South Ryegate, Vermont.

KINGFISHER

CHICKADEE

BLUEBIR

CARDINAL

NUTHATCH

WOODPEC

THRASHER

ROBIN [THRUSH]

OWLS

TURKEY

QUAIL

PHEASANT

ROADRUNNER

PIGEON

BARN SWALLOW

DOVE

CAVE SWALLOW

HUMMINGBIRD

TREE SWALLOW

WREN

LOON

GREBE

GOOSE

DUCK

SWAN